IMAGES
of America

MITCHELL COUNTY

The art of photography took off in earnest with the start of the 20th century. Many individuals bought cameras and set themselves up as part-time "picture men." Some established small studios. Others traveled around with their cameras to different local communities. Pictured here is photographer Jim Jones, a Bakersville resident, who captured many of the images within this book. (Courtesy of Daniel Barron.)

IMAGES
of America

MITCHELL
COUNTY

Michael C. Hardy

ARCADIA
PUBLISHING

Published by Arcadia Publishing
Charleston, South Carolina

Library of Congress Catalog Card Number: 2008932682

For all general information contact Arcadia Publishing at:
Telephone 843-853-2070
Fax 843-853-0044
E-mail sales@arcadiapublishing.com
For customer service and orders:
Toll-Free 1-888-313-2665

Visit us on the Internet at www.arcadiapublishing.com

*To all of those Mitchell County people
who have saved little bits of their families' histories.
Thanks for sharing.*

CONTENTS

ACKNOWLEDGMENTS

Thanks go out to many people for making this project possible. The author would like to extend his deepest appreciation to Daniel Barron, George and Robby Morgan, Buster and Irene Sparks, Chris Hollifield, David Biddix, and Rhonda Gunter. This project would not have been possible without them and their generous help and support. Thanks also go out to the Mitchell County Historical Society, the Bakersville Public Library, and the Spruce Pine Public Library for allowing me to meet the public and scan photographs. Also I thank the *Mitchell News-Journal* for the helpful articles. And the author wishes to thank his editor, Maggie Bullwinkel, for all her help. As always, this book would not have been possible without the love and support (and proofreading) of Elizabeth Baird Hardy.

INTRODUCTION

Mitchell County shares its name with four other counties in the United States. The one in Georgia is named for a Revolutionary War soldier; the one in Texas takes its name from two brothers who were Texas revolutionaries; Iowa's Mitchell County is named after an Irish patriot; and the Mitchell County in Kansas was named in honor of a Union officer killed in the Civil War. North Carolina's Mitchell County is the only one not named for a soldier. Our county was named for a University of North Carolina professor killed in his attempts to measure the highest peak east of the Mississippi River.

Dr. Elisha Mitchell first visited the area in 1835, taking measurements in the Black Mountains. One peak in particular, then called Black Dome, was measured at 6,672 feet. Dr. Mitchell returned several times, confirming his measurements. In the 1850s, a dispute arose when one of his former students, Senator Thomas L. Clingman, took his own measurements in the Black Mountains. Clingman claimed that Mitchell had measured the wrong peak, and that, in fact, he himself had correctly determined the highest mountain. Mitchell returned to the area in 1857 to confirm his earlier investigations. While hiking alone, he slipped and fell to his death. His body was found in a waterfall by legendary tracker and hunter Big Tom Wilson.

There were settlers in the area long before Dr. Mitchell met his tragic end and provided the namesake for the future county. In 1790, the Toe River Valley population numbered 80 families, including the Brights, Wisemans, and Bakers. They were soon followed by the Silver, Buchanan, Griffin, Bailey, and Ellis families.

The early 1830s marked the first events to place a regional and national spotlight onto the area destined to become Mitchell County: the tragic deaths of Charlie and Frances "Frankie" (Stewart) Silver. There are many stories about the Silvers, all of which contain some level of truth. It is, however, difficult to untangle the tales and find the facts. Charlie and Frankie were a young married couple living with their infant daughter near the North Toe River in the present- day community of Kona. One evening, near Christmas 1831, Charlie allegedly came home intoxicated and commenced to beat Frankie. Fearing for her life, and for that of her little girl, Frankie fought back, mortally wounding Charlie with an ax blow to the head. Lacking knowledge about the legal system of the time, Frankie attempted to cover up her crime of self-defense. After several days, Charlie's kinfolks began to suspect something was amiss. Parts of the body were found in the fireplace and other parts in a hollow log in the woods. Frankie was arrested, imprisoned in Morganton, and tried for the murder of her husband. Given the fact that defendants in capital cases were not allowed to testify in their own defense during that period of history, Frankie was found guilty and sentenced to death without telling her side of the story. With the help of her family, she escaped once but was recaptured, and on July 12, 1833, she was hanged in Morganton. The remains of Charlie lie in the cemetery at the Kona Cemetery. Frankie was buried outside Morganton. Very few histories of Appalachia or volumes on folklore do not mention this story or one of its variations.

The formation of Mitchell County was as turbulent as the time period in which the county was formed. As early as 1853, according to a contemporary Asheville newspaper, there were people in Yancey County trying to get a new county formed. It was not until 1860 that they succeeded.

In January 1861, a new county named Mitchell was formed from portions of Yancey, Watauga, Caldwell, Burke, and McDowell Counties. The new county ran, as described in its charter, "from the top of Grand Father Mountain, with the old Watauga line, to the Blue Ridge . . . [then] to stop on the Toe River, at the mouth of Big Rock Creek, thence with the big ridge that divides Rock Creek and Brummett's Creek to the State line at the point where the Yancey and McDowell turnpike road crosses said line." A set of commissioners was appointed to select a permanent seat of justice and to secure 50 acres to start a town. The commissioners had only two months to fulfill their charge. According to the record, a "hitch" occurred somewhere, and a second set of commissioners was chosen. These men were given more time, between October 1, 1861, and July 1, 1862, to select a new county seat. On October 17, 1861, Lysander Childs and Eben Childs donated 50 acres of land "for the location thereon of a permanent seat of justice." Their donation included "two acres for a public grave-yard, one acre for the site of a public school building, and one acre" for churches, to include "Episcopalians, Presbyterians, Methodist and Baptist." The new town was the site of Childsville, which was probably not more than a building or two, including a post office. The name of the community was changed to Calhoun in honor of statesman and vice president John C. Calhoun. Court was held in Calhoun beginning in June 1861.

Not everyone was happy with the location of the new county seat. "The justices of the peace refused to levy taxes for the erection of the courthouse at Calhoun," according to one state history, saying that "it was inconvenient to three-fourths of the citizens." The matter was referred to the general assembly, and residents of Mitchell County were authorized to choose, by ballot, between Calhoun and another spot known as Davis. An additional act was passed in 1863, stating the county should be surveyed and the geographical center chosen as the county seat. The commissioners met and chose Norman's Hill as the site. In 1866, the commissioners met again and started laying out lots for a town, but in 1868, the county seat was moved to Bakersville, which was incorporated in 1870. The county parameters remained much the same until 1911, when part of the northeastern section of the county was taken to create Avery County.

All of the wrangling regarding the establishment of the county and the location of a seat of justice took place during the tumultuous years of the American Civil War. The war undoubtedly contributed to the instability of the area. Men from the county served on both sides of the conflict, with 60 percent serving in the Confederate army. One historian once wrote, "Mitchell Co. families suffered horribly during the War, not only from lack of food but from lawless elements who hid among the isolated hills and valleys and preyed upon the innocent." While no large-scale battles were fought in Mitchell County, the war had a profound effect on all its residents: those men who survived combat often returned home maimed in body and spirit, while civilians at home suffered from privation and the depredations of outliers, scoundrels, and soldiers from both armies. The mistrust and resentment engendered by the war lasted for generations.

Two industrial forces have come to epitomize Mitchell County's economic and social history: the mining of mica and the arrival of the railroad.

Long before European settlement, even before fabled Spanish explorers, the Cherokee and their ancestors mined the area for mica and other precious gems. As evidence of the presence of these early miners, Native American artifacts have been found at several sites in Mitchell County, most notably the Sink Hole Mine near Bandana and the Horse Stamp Mine on Rich's Knob. The Cherokee had in their oral tradition in the 19th century that "companies of white men came on mules from the south, worked during the summer, and carried off a white metal with them." The legend may refer to Spanish explorers who came to the region in search of silver and other precious resources.

It would not be until after the Civil War that a market was found for mica. Later in his life, former Confederate soldier Zac McHone recalled taking a piece of mica to sell in Marion in 1870. Near that same time, Elisha B. Clapp came to Mitchell County and began working in local mines, like the Sink Hole Mine. Clapp and his partner, John G. Heap, manufactured and sold "House-Furnishing Goods" in Knoxville. They discovered that mica sheets could be used as windows on their stoves. Mining was soon in full force in the county. In 1892, mica from Mitchell County's Ray

Mine was exhibited with some fanfare at the World's Fair in Vienna. In 1878, Thomas Edison began using mica in electric motors and later in his phonographs. The world now had a need for mica, and Mitchell County stepped up its production. During the war years of the early 20th century, mica was heavily mined in the area, and mica could be found in every electrical component in every airplane, truck, and tank, as well as in the eyeholes of gas masks, road goggles, and armored car peepholes. It could also be found in paint, wallpaper, roofing, and lubricants.

Mica, however, was not the only resource mined in Mitchell County. Iron ore was mined at Cranberry, which was a part of Mitchell County from 1861 until 1911. Beryl, emeralds, and aquamarine were also mined, as was feldspar. Feldspar has been used as a cleaning powder and as a component in ceramics in the electrical industry, cookware, pottery, tile, and glass. It also gives strength to the "lead" used in pencils. There were mines all over Mitchell County throughout the 20th century. Production plants were located in Spruce Pine and Toecane, and the finished product was transported out via the railroad.

Prior to the arrival of the railroad, exporting large quantities of mica and feldspar was impossible. Wagoners had to negotiate rough roads with their teams and heavy loads. As early as the 1830s, people had envisioned a route from Charleston, South Carolina, to Cincinnati, Ohio. In 1836, work began, but only 18 miles of track were completed. Nearly 50 years passed, and while there was much talk, a passage across the Blue Ridge Mountains was never completed. In 1887, the Charleston, Cincinnati, and Chicago Railroad was organized. This company was sold in 1893 and then again in 1902. The line became known as the South and Western Railroad. By 1905, the rails had reached as far as Spruce Pine. That year, the line stretching from Elkhorn City, Kentucky, to Spruce Pine was sold and reorganized as the Carolina, Clinchfield, and Ohio Railroad, commonly known as the Clinchfield. Work continued on the line, and by 1915, track was completed to Spartanburg, South Carolina. The line was later acquired by CSX. At a distance of 277 miles, the Clinchfield is the shortest connecting line between the Ohio River and South Carolina. Forty-two percent of the mainline is on a curve, and 55 tunnels are scattered along the entire line. The highest point on the line is at Altapass, at 2,629 feet above sea level. The line has been called "the greatest railroad engineering feat of the Twentieth Century." Even today, the line hauls the majority of coal from the coalfields of central Appalachia to the Eastern Seaboard. When Mitchell County was being heavily mined for minerals, they were shipped out on the Clinchfield to points all across the United States.

Towns such as Toecane, Spruce Pine, and Altapass bloomed overnight. Hotels, inns, and boardinghouses were opened to accommodate the visitors who flocked to the area. The hotel at Altapass had a bowling alley. In Spruce Pine, there was a theater. There was also a theater in Bakersville. The railroad had bypassed the county seat by three miles, and other towns in the county quickly took precedence.

Numerous spur lines were built, connecting with the Clinchfield at various points along the line. There was a spur line from the head of Brushy Fork, where the Wiseman mine was located, that ran into the Harris facility. The Black Mountain Railway ran out of Kona and into Yancey County. At Huntdale, the Caney River Railway ran west to Bald Mountain in Yancey County. Then there was the Crabtree Creek Railroad, running through Newdale. These lines were quite short-lived, existing only long enough to exploit the minerals in the ground or the forests that grew on top of them. Once these resources were depleted, the lines were taken up.

Mitchell County was quickly becoming a popular tourist destination. Visitors could come in on the Clinchfield, stay at one of the local hotels, and visit the many wonders the county had to offer. One of those locales was Roan Mountain, on the northern edge of the county. Locals and visitors alike traveled up the Roan and took in the natural beauty and the commanding views. Trout fishing in the Linville, Toe, and Cane Rivers was also popular.

In 1911, the northern part of Mitchell County, containing the Linville Falls community, Cranberry, and Grandfather Mountain, was formed into a new county: Avery. Avery was the last county created in the state of North Carolina; Mitchell's borders have remained unchanged since that time.

Throughout the 20th century, Mitchell County has on several occasions risen to the forefront of events in the state. In 1923, Lucy Morgan, a teacher at the Appalachian School in Penland, established the Penland Weavers. The program taught local women how to weave, an art that had been all but lost in the mountains of Western North Carolina. Many traditional artistic practices had dwindled with the availability of cheap, ready-made textiles and other goods, all brought in on the railroad. In the early 20th century, however, there was a national resurgence of interest in items made by hand with traditional techniques. At times, looms and materials were provided, and Morgan helped the women in marketing their handicrafts. The Penland School still exists to this day, instructing more than 1,000 students a year in book- and paper-making, clay, drawing, glassblowing, metal smithing, photography, textiles, and woodworking.

In 1937, the Carolina Theater was built. While it provided local entertainment with the showing of the latest movies, it also became the home for the nationally broadcast *Carolina Barn Dance*. Every Saturday night, musicians, both local and national acts, came to play in Spruce Pine. The program was broadcast to more than 500 different radio stations in the United States. Some of the acts included Toe River Valley's own Lulu Belle and Scotty, as well as Patsy Cline, Bill Monroe, and Kitty Wells. The *Barn Dance* went off the air in the mid-1950s, but the theater still stands; it is being restored and is offering concerts once again.

In 1909, there was talk of, and a little work on, a road known as the "Crest of the Blue Ridge Highway." The road was to be 24 feet wide with a sand-clay or gravel surface, and it was intended to connect Marion, Virginia, to Cornelia, Georgia. Boone, Blowing Rock, Grandfather Mountain, Linville, and Little Switzerland were just a few of the places the road passed through. Elements of the road can still be seen today by those who know where to look. While the road was never completed, it gave rise to another road: the Blue Ridge Parkway. The parkway was built to connect the Shenandoah National Park with the Great Smoky Mountains National Park. Construction was begun on September 11, 1935, and the project was finished 52 years later. The 469-mile road covers two states: Virginia and North Carolina. The southern border of Mitchell County is traversed by the parkway.

There are countless other glimpses of Mitchell County history that could be given here. Roan Mountain to the north, along with the Appalachian Trail, has its own unique history. There is the Mineral Museum along the parkway. Then there are the Overmountain Men, the annual Mineral and Gem Festival, the Rhododendron Festival, and many other events that make Mitchell County a special place.

Within the pages of this book are many glimpses of Mitchell County's past, its people, and its places. These glimpses have captured a fraction of a second, hardly a blink of an eye in the lives of the people and places frozen in each image, but they each tell a piece of a wonderful story of life in a beautiful land.

One

FROM THE ROAN
TO GILLESPIE GAP
CHURCH AND COMMUNITY

The death of a family member has always brought the community together. Male members of the community made the coffin, while the women washed and dressed the body, often constructing the shroud. Family and friends would "sit up" overnight with the deceased, and food was brought in abundance. This photograph depicts a burial in the late 19th century at the cemetery connected with the Lily Branch Baptist Church. (Courtesy of Jerry Sullins.)

The date written on the back of this photograph, 1895, makes this one of the earliest known photographs of Bakersville. At center is the second Bakersville Court House. It occupies the same position as the 1907 courthouse, although the 1907 structure faces south. On the right side, with arched windows, is the Bakersville Methodist Church. (Courtesy of Daniel Barron.)

Singing schools were held at churches throughout the United States in the late 19th century and through the first half of the 20th century, offering valuable musical instruction to communities where such lessons may have been otherwise hard to acquire. This singing school, with students of all ages, was held at McKinney's Cove Baptist Church in the 1940s. (Courtesy of Rhonda Gunter.)

Two stories have been handed down regarding the naming of Booneford. Some think it is named for famed explorer and hunter Daniel Boone, who reportedly forded the North Toe River near the town. Another story is that the community was named for Robert Boone, a Confederate soldier and local citizen. The railroad depot can be seen at the top of this 1956 photograph. (Courtesy of John L. Burn.)

The switchboard operator was a well-known person to the folks in Mitchell County; all calls had to go through the switchboard. In this photograph, taken in 1951, Lillie Lou Young is filling in for the normal operator, Mattie Greene. The switchboard was located on the upper floor of the Jim Greene building. (Courtesy of Daniel Barron.)

For 38 years, Rev. Charles McKinney pastored the McKinney Cove Baptist Church. Pay for a pastor during the late 19th and early 20th centuries was often difficult. At times, his parishioners paid his salary with money, poultry, or produce from their gardens. McKinney is pictured here with his granddaughter Edith Byrd and his wife, Sarah Singleton McKinney. (Courtesy of Rhonda Gunter.)

Not many folks in Mitchell County know there is more than one Crabtree Falls in the area. This postcard from the 1920s shows the other Crabtree Falls, upstream from the popular one on the Blue Ridge Parkway and located on private property. (Courtesy of Emerald Village.)

Members of Beaver Creek Baptist Church are here pictured around 1939: from left to right (first row) Howard Gunter, Carl Pitman, Nina Swann, Emma Swann, Nina Burleson, Norian Grindstaff, Louise Carpenter, unidentified, Faye Burleson, Louise Henline, Phyllis Henline, Margarot McGee, Wado Hise, and Betty McGee; (second row) Charlie Woody, R. J. Swann, Glenn Hise, Ira Burleson, ? Sullins, Vivian Carpenter, Grace Pitman, Grace Swann, Sam Ellis, Lewis Burleson, Hoyle Gunter, Jack Carpenter, Lewis Pitman, Ray Woody, unidentified, Gertrude Henline (holding baby), and Mary Heline McGee; (third row) Glennie Stamey, Kathleen Freeman, Sally Henline (holding baby), ? Hise, ? Freeman, Ina Grindstaff, unidentified, Rosa Hise, Marginia Buchanan, Ruth Pittman, and Beadulah Hise; (fourth row) ? Lyons, Len Freeman, Mark Swann, Florence Buchanan, Bert Pendley, Homer Buchanan, Lonnie Gunter, Doyle Gunter, unidentified, Ada Gunter, Bertie Gunter, Monroe Stamey, Homer Hise, Mitt Swann, and Frank Swann. (Courtesy of Russell and Mary Burleson.)

The Buladean community started out as Wilder, named after John Wilder, the general who owned the Cloudland Hotel and numerous mines. The name was then changed to Magnetic City in the late 1800s because of the number of mines. Later a new name was chosen. A favorite song at the time was the gospel number "Beulah Land," and Buladean became the name of the town. Here Bill Hill stands with the Buladean Presbyterian Church in the background. (Courtesy of Claudia McGough.)

Due to persecution, members of the Church of the Brethren began immigrating to the New World prior to 1750. The first congregation was established in Germantown, Pennsylvania, in 1723. The group sent out missionaries, quickly establishing churches and spreading about the colonies. This photograph shows women at the annual conference at Brummett's Creek in 1913. (Courtesy of Rhonda Gunter.)

Situated on the Mitchell/Yancey County border, Crabtree Falls has been a popular site for tourists, both locals and "off-mountainers," for many decades. Prior to the building of the Blue Ridge Parkway, there were several crab apple orchards. While the orchards are now gone, many trees still remain. The 70-foot falls drop over hundreds of small ledges, creating a dramatic effect. (Courtesy of Chris Hollifield.)

In 1925, the congregation of the Bakersville Baptist Church decided to build a new church. Plans were acquired, and the property was purchased from the Flemming family. Church member Charles Greene worked hard for the new structure, telling people, "Everybody a part; each child a brick." The brick building was finished in 1928, and the congregation gathered on the steps during the dedication for this photograph. (Courtesy of the Morgan family.)

According to local tradition, the name "Loafer's Glory" was coined by the women of the community who took a dim view of the men's habit of "lollygagging" on the porch of the local store rather than taking part in working or other gainful employment. Thus the community became a "loafer's glory." This 1950s view from a postcard shows three of the community's namesakes. (Courtesy of the Morgan family.)

Books have always been highly prized additions to a home. Prof. Charles Wing established a library at his school in Ledger, and later Mitchell County gained its first public library. In the 1940s, a bookmobile was purchased. The bookmobile was able to take a small selection of books into the community and lend these books to citizens who might not be able to travel to libraries in Mitchell County. (Courtesy of the Morgan family.)

Bear Creek Baptist Church was the third Baptist church established in what would become Mitchell County. The church was constituted in 1830. The fellowship's first building was made of logs and had a dirt floor. This building was constructed in 1891 and served as the place where worshippers gathered until 1926, when it was replaced. (Courtesy of Buster Sparks.)

There was a post office in the community of Mica from the 1870s until 1938, when it was discontinued. This building was constructed in 1914 and served as both a store and a post office until 1938. Mitchell County resident Calvin Hall rescued, moved, and restored the building. (Courtesy of Michael C. Hardy.)

Clarence Buchanan, seen here baptizing a member of Bear Creek Baptist Church, was ordained a pastor at Bear Creek on May 23, 1931. Julius Henline preached at his ordination. At one time, Buchanan pastored six different churches at once, not an uncommon practice in the mid-20th century. (Courtesy of Buster Sparks.)

At the mention of the name of Rev. Bruce Buchanan, most folks will exclaim that he was a "great man of God," a fitting tribute. Buchanan pastored several churches in the area, including Roan Mountain Baptist Church and Pine Branch Baptist Church. He is pictured here at Pine Branch in the 1940s. (Courtesy of Louellen Peterson.)

Some communities, such as Toecane, Spruce Pine, and Altapass, thrived with the coming of the railroad. While the railroad never came to Bakersville proper, the community flourished as a result of nearby rail service, as shown in this 1920s photograph. Businesses included George M. Young and Sons Groceries and the Merchants and Farmers Bank. (Courtesy of Mitchell County Historical Society.)

Around 1870, a group gathered to organize a Methodist church in Bakersville. Many members of this group of believers had come to Bakersville to work in the budding mica industry. The Reverend G. W. Martin was appointed by the Holston Conference as the first pastor of the new church. Pictured here are the members of the Bakersville Methodist Church sometime after 1929. (Courtesy of Louellen Peterson.)

Born in 1860 in Yancey County, Rev. John A. Gouge was a well-known and loved pastor and teacher. Gouge was pastor at Lily Branch Baptist Church for many years and also served as moderator of the Mitchell County Baptist Association in 1914. He was married to Huldah Thomas. John Gouge died in 1937. (Courtesy of the Morgan family.)

Taken in 1956, this image depicts the men's Sunday school class of Roan Mountain Baptist Church. From left to right are (first row) Guy Hobson, Vance McKinney, Gordon Young, Claude Young, and unidentified; (second row) two unidentified, Herman McKinney, Vernan McKinney, Oscar Greene, Leslie Greene, John Wilson, Ed Greene, Joe Young, Mos Young, and unidentified. (Courtesy of Darlene Wise.)

There is not much to Spruce Pine in this 1903 photograph, taken about the same time the South and Western Railway was completed. For a time, Spruce Pine was the end of the line. A depot is in the center of the photograph, and great stacks of lumber stand ready for use, possibly as railroad ties or for shipping, beside the tracks. (Courtesy of Rhonda Gunter.)

In 1926, Bear Creek Baptist Church built a new sanctuary. This building, pictured above, had arched (or Gothic) windows and served until 1959, when a new sanctuary was constructed beside the old one. The old building was covered in brick and now serves as offices, Sunday school rooms, and a museum dedicated to church history. (Courtesy of Buster Sparks.)

Texie Greene is pictured during her annual apple-butter making at her Bear Creek farm. Like many Mitchell County women, Texie used a variety of methods to preserve the products of a relatively short growing season. Apple butter requires hours of cooking and nearly constant stirring to produce a quality preserve. Texie had a special kettle she used each year to produce her apple butter. Such kettles are frequently family heirlooms. (Courtesy of Debra Cagle.)

The Little Switzerland Resort area was established in 1909. A year later, a 25-room hotel, the Switzerland Inn, opened. The inn was designed by Charlotte architect Louis H. Asbury and was covered with chestnut bark in much the same way as the Eseeola Inn in Avery County was finished. The inn was torn down in 1970, and a new inn with the same name was constructed. (Courtesy of Pack Memorial Library.)

For the vast majority of Mitchell County churches, baptism was an outdoor practice until the late 20th century, and some churches still baptize in creeks or streams rather than in indoor baptisteries. When candidates for baptism included women, children, or young adults, deacons would frequently be stationed downstream to catch anyone who might slip through the preacher's hands. (Courtesy of Rhonda Gunter.)

Prior to the advent of radio, telephones, television, and the Internet, the only forms of communication were visitors and newspapers. In the 19th century, newspapers came from Asheville, Salisbury, and Raleigh. Bakersville, the county seat, was incorporated in 1870 and gained its first post office in 1874. Prior to 1874, post offices existed in Childsville, also known as Calhoun, and in Cranberry. (Courtesy of Daniel Barron.)

Travel writer David Dudley Warner, writing in 1888, called Bakersville "a pretty place in the hills, of some six hundred inhabitants." Bakersville was incorporated in 1870 as the county seat of Mitchell County. This early image shows the 1907 courthouse in the center of the photograph and the Methodist church south on a hill to the left of the courthouse. (Courtesy of the Mitchell County Historical Society.)

These fine folks, members of the Roan Mountain Baptist Church, have gathered for a revival. Pastor Julius Henline wrote this on the back of the photograph: "One of the greatest meetings of my ministry. So many members 16 for baptism and a number of conversions from other places. My seventh year as Pastor of Roan Mtn. Baptist Church." (Courtesy of Darlene Wise.)

Baptist Church
Bakersville, N.C.

A revival in 1869 led to the formation of the Bakersville Baptist Church. The congregation met in the courthouse. By the end of the 1870s, a building was erected in downtown Bakersville. The flood of 1901 washed away this building, with the "bell tolling a farewell," according to church history. The second building was erected soon thereafter on Black Street on property donated by the Black family. The new building had a raised platform and wooden benches. In 1925, the decision was made to erect a new brick building, pictured here after the completion of the church in 1928. The Reverend Charles G. Ellis was pastor at the time. A new steeple was added not long ago, and a century-old bell still peals the call for worshippers to come and gather. (Courtesy of Daniel Barron.)

Singing schools were frequently one of the few annual highlights for a community. Traveling teachers came to teach students how to sing, often using music books with shape notes. Young people sometimes used these social occasions to further their courtships. Often a photographer would come the last day of the school and take a picture of the teacher and his class at the location where the class was held. This photograph was taken at Bear Creek Baptist Church in 1913. (Courtesy of Buster Sparks.)

On May 20, 1920, Pastor Stephen Morgan Greene of Roan Mountain Baptist Church met his congregation on the banks of Cane Creek. They were there to observe the sacred ordinance of baptism. Several individuals came forward for baptism, including these two earnest young men. Walter Raleigh Young stands to the right of Reverend Greene. (Courtesy of Darlene Wise.)

What is now known as the Church of the Brethren began in Germany in 1708. Brethren beliefs were largely the same as those of other Protestants, differing only on the idea that Jesus taught that we should live a different kind of life, one based on "peaceful action, plain and compassionate living, and a shared search for truth." This photograph shows the Church of the Brethren on Brummett's Creek. (Courtesy of Rhonda Gunter.)

The first couple of decades in the 20th century brought incredible growth to Toecane. The depot was open day and night. There were eight stores, a church, a barbershop, a school, a restaurant, a soda fountain, and two hotels, not to mention Blevins's Oil Company and Southern Feldspar. Here in the 1900s, local citizens have gathered to welcome the first passenger train into Toecane. (Courtesy of the Mitchell County Historical Society.)

The Big McKinney Feldspar Mine is featured in this June 1946 image. Large-scale production had already ceased at the mine when this photograph was taken. A few smaller operations were coming in to "cobb spar" from the mine. A sense of the mine opening's size can be gained by noticing how it dwarfs the truck at the bottom left of the mine entrance. The Big McKinney, along with the Bon Ami mine, became the local attraction the Emerald Village in 1979. (Courtesy of Emerald Village.)

Roan Mountain Baptist Church is the third oldest Baptist church in Mitchell County. The church's first building was a log cabin with dirt floors and a hole in the roof to vent smoke from an open-pit fire. This photograph, taken around 1872, shows parishioners beside their frame-constructed building. (Courtesy of Darlene Wise.)

Denominational groups in Mitchell County, such as Baptist, Methodist, and Presbyterian, usually have a yearly conference. This photograph shows a conference held at the Brummett's Creek Church of the Brethren in 1913. The subjects' somber expressions are not necessarily a reflection of their religious beliefs; early photographic technology required individuals to sit as still as possible, and holding a smile is difficult. (Courtesy of Rhonda Gunter.)

A visitor traveling this road to the Big McKinney Mine in the 1950s would have met a variety of trucks and other vehicles going back and forth to the mines. This photograph was taken in 1964 after large-scale mining operations had ceased. (Courtesy of Emerald Village.)

Jonathan Duncan was born in 1832. He pastored a number of Baptist churches in the Toe River Valley, including Crabtree (1849). In 1885, he was called to be the first pastor of the Silver Chapel Baptist Church. In 1910, he was pastoring in Penland. Duncan died in 1915. (Courtesy of Rhonda Gunter.)

This building, the second used by the Pine Branch Baptist Church, served as their sanctuary from 1920 until 1948, when a new church was built on a hill behind this structure. (Courtesy of Louellen Peterson.)

The Reverend Thomas Blalock (seated, center) lived from 1865 until 1960. Over the course of his long life, he served as a Baptist missionary to China for 56 years, publishing a book about his evangelical experiences in 1949. He was married three times, the first time in China to Emma Humpries; his second and third wives were Mae Lilly Cornwall and Leola Woodley, respectively. (Courtesy of Rhonda Gunter.)

Somewhere around this point, near the community of Relief, the North Toe River becomes the Nolichucky River. The Nolichucky continues on its journey north and west, and eventually it flows into the Mississippi River and the Gulf of Mexico. (Courtesy of Michael C. Hardy.)

Beekeeping has traditionally been important to Mitchell County not only for honey production, but also primarily for the valuable pollination the bees provide. While bees are not native to North America, they quickly became established after their introduction by early settlers. Many of the area's essential crops, like apples, depend upon the pollination of honeybees. Historically, Mitchell County residents might "rob" a tree in the wild to acquire honey or to domesticate the bees. These proud beekeepers, G. B. Barnett (left) and Edd Bennett, have well-made hives, some with removable frames to aid in honey harvesting. Also, like many veteran beekeepers, they are not wearing veils or gloves since they are not actually disturbing a hive. The relationship between a beekeeper and the bees is so important that mountain tradition holds that the bees must be told when a family member dies or they will fly away and never return. (Courtesy of Rhonda Gunter.)

Two

SCHOOLHOUSE, SPORTS, AND STUDENTS
EDUCATION

In 1936, the Tipton Hill boys' basketball team played the team from Mars Hill for the championship and was victorious. Pictured from left to right are (first row) coach Harry Shawford, Howard Gouge, Gene Griffith, Leonard Tipton, and mascot A. J. Jarrett; (second row) Buck Buchanan, Lonzo Roberts, George Roberts, Howard McKinney, and Edward Proffitt. (Courtesy of Cynthia Burleson.)

From the early 1900s until 1978, Harris High School in Spruce Pine prepared students for life and higher education. This sign, pictured with Julia Burleson on the left and Joe Carpenter on the right, greeted hundreds of students during the 1960s. Today a gymnasium in a high school is foregone conclusion, but in the 1960s, it was something to boast about on the school sign. (Courtesy of Chris Hollifield.)

There have been several different institutions that have born the name "Bowman," always in honor of J. Clayton Bowman. The first was the Bowman Academy, established in the 1870s. The academy later became the Mitchell Collegiate Institute. In the 1920s, the property was purchased by the county and, in 1922, became the Mitchell County High School. In 1929, the name was changed to Bowman High School. (Courtesy of the Morgan family.)

Loafer's Glory might have earned its name from the loafing that took place there, but its residents were concerned with education. This framed building, clean and freshly painted, served the students of the area until consolidation started to take place. (Courtesy of the Morgan family.)

Bowman High School's cheerleaders in 1958 were, from left to right, (first row) Judy Phillips, Sandra Snyder, Sallie Graham (captain), Amelia Webb, and Ethel Forbes; (second row) Gail McKinney, Myrtle Ruth Duncan, Shelby Snynder (cocaptain), Linda McKinney, and Donald Willis. (Courtesy of the Morgan family.)

Many people across Mitchell County still speak fondly of Professor Wing. Born in Boston, Massachusetts, in August 1836, Charles Hallack Wing was a chemistry professor at Cornell University and at the Massachusetts Institute of Technology (MIT). He resigned from MIT and moved to Mitchell County. Wing built a large log home, along with blacksmith and carpenter shops. Wing is probably best known for his school, the Wing Academy, and a 27,000-volume library, known as the Good-Will Library. It is rumored Wing actually offered people 50¢ a day to attend the school. One local man remembered people showing up with large hemp sacks to take books from the library. Books were seldom lost or not returned. Wing's ill health and the unification of the public school system caused the demise of the Wing Academy. The school was closed, and Wing returned to Boston. He died in 1915 and was buried at the Bear Creek Baptist Church in Mitchell County. The photograph above shows Professor Wing driving an early automobile. (Courtesy of the Morgan family.)

Given its closeness to Spruce Pine and Alta Pass, Harris High School has always been a large institution. Shown here are two c. 1947 eighth-grade classes. Many eighth-grade and high school graduating classes, instead of using caps and gowns, opted for matching dress clothes. Girls would select a fabric and pattern and make their own dresses, so they match but are still unique. (Courtesy of Russell and Mary Burleson.)

In the early 1920s, the residents of Tipton Hill felt the need for a school. They raised funds and started construction. The school was quickly purchased by the county. In 1929, the school was described as having "steam heat, electric lights, drinking fountains, and a . . . sewage system." The WPA soon constructed a rock building for a high school, and this brick building was used for the elementary grades. The building was torn down in 1959 to make way for a new gymnasium and lunchroom. (Courtesy of the Morgan family.)

The Latin Club at Harris High School was obviously a popular organization. From left to right are (first row) Wayne Ellis, president; Jackie Rose, reporter; Angie Burleson, secretary; Jeri Sullins, treasurer; Frances Riddle; and Dale Duncan, vice president; (second row) Mrs. ? Arnold, sponsor; Judy Buchanan; Louise Buchanan; Marie Hall; Barbara Boone; Alice Self; Jane Wiseman; and Jimmy Young; (third row) Earl Pitman; Winston Hefner; Marvin Woody; Larry M. Sparks; David Dayton; Danny McKinney; and Michael Shipman. (Courtesy of Chris Hollifield.)

Students of all ages were taught at the one-room schoolhouse at the head of Beaver Creek. One-room schoolhouses were once common, and it must have been quite a feat for the teacher, often a young woman, to teach children ranging from first graders to high school students. The noise emerging from these schools led to their being called "blab schools." (Courtesy of Rhonda Gunter.)

The first public high school in Spruce Pine was established about the same time the town was incorporated: 1907. As the town grew, so did the need for a new school. Mining leader C. J. Harris donated property for a new school in 1916 and asked that it be named in honor of his brother. The school was therefore christened the Dr. William Torrey Harris Memorial High School. (Courtesy of Rhonda Gunter.)

The 1924 Bowman High School girls' basketball team featured, from left to right, Geneva Phillips, coach; Viela Wilson, center; Elizabeth Lawson, forward; Stella Anderson, forward; Sallie Hobson, guard; Dollie Bowman, guard; and Helen McBee, forward. (Courtesy of the Morgan family.)

The members of the award-winning 1929 boys' basketball team from Bowman High School in Bakersville were, from left to right, principal Jamel L. Burnette, coach Essie Gouge, Frank Phillips, Love Hughes, Lane Wilson, Audie Silvers, unidentified, Harry Phillips, Harry Greene, Fred Stanley, Richard Baker, and George Willis. (Courtesy of the Morgan family.)

Renus Rich, pictured here, was a traveling singing school teacher. These teachers traveled around the country leading singing schools at churches for all ages. Rich was also a small part of the Johnson City recording sessions, which took place in Johnson City, Tennessee, between 1928 and 1929. Columbia Records recorded Rich and Carl Bradshaw singing "Goodbye Sweetheart" and "Sleep Baby Sleep" on October 15, 1928. (Courtesy of Buster Sparks.)

In the early 19th century, education was provided by parents at home or by hired tutors. Following the Civil War, the idea of a free education came to pass, and "free schools" were established. Any child in the community could attend the six- or eight-week program. Following the free portion of the class, the teacher would stay on for a subscription school for those who could afford to pay the teacher's salary. These school programs could last up to six months. The building above is the free school building in Bakersville. Teachers included Pearl Pritchard, Clara Lambert, and Gene McKinney. The school was located on Hanry Ledford's property. (Courtesy of Bud McKinney.)

Originally known as the Bowman Academy, the Mitchell Collegiate Institute was operated by the Home Mission Board of the Southern Baptist Convention from the late 1800s until 1923, when it was purchased by the Mitchell County School Board. In 1929, the name was changed to Bowman High School in honor of education pioneer J. Clayton Bowman. (Courtesy of the Morgan family.)

Roan Mountain had an exceptionally well-built and large school in the 1920s. Pictured on the porch are three of the school's teachers: from left to right, Lou Conley, Jeter Burleson, and Carrie Young. (Courtesy of Rhonda Gunter.)

The Harris High School boys' and girls' basketball teams were photographed together around 1925. In the very front is team mascot Edward Warrick Jr. From left to right are (first row) Georgia Wright, Lillian Turbyfield, Ruth Loven, Nola Houpe, Marjorie Ward, Grace Davenport, Maude Young, and unknown; (second row) ? Warrick (coach), Frank Ellis, Milton Young, Lee Swann, Beverly Loven, Jack Tappan, Edd Swann, Brown Buchanan, and Dr. Jack Burleson (assistant coach). (Courtesy of Russell and Mary Burleson.)

Girls of the Mitchell Collegiate Institute of Bakersville posed for this image in 1912. From left to right are (first row) Inez Black, Pauline Baker (Poteat), Mauda McKinney (Hensley), Frances Burleson (Randolph), and Ethel Wilson (Blevins); (second row) Georgia Dodson, Edith Young (McKinney), Estelle Burleson, Eleanor Teague (Baker), Margaret Teague, Viola Phillips, and Mrs. R. T. (Margaret) Teague. (Courtesy of Chris Hollifield.)

Students at the Appalachian Industrial School, an Episcopal mission school established around 1911, pose in front of the Farm House, originally owned by the Conley family. The Reverend Rufus Morgan served as one of the mission school's early directors. It was Morgan's sister, Lucy, who expanded this vision through the founding of the Penland Weavers and Potters, a community-based weaving and craft cooperative that provided income to the families in the Penland area. Out of the Penland Weavers and Potters would emerge the Penland School of Crafts. (Courtesy of Penland School of Crafts.)

Baseball was a popular sport across the country in the 20th century, and Mitchell County was no exception. In 1924, the baseball team of Bowman High School posed for this image. Excluding their coach and batboy, the team only had nine players, ensuring a full game of play for all members. (Courtesy of the Morgan family.)

The Little Poplar School was originally a one-room schoolhouse in the Poplar community. It was moved to the grounds of the Mitchell County High School as a reminder of what education use to be like more than 100 years ago in Mitchell County. Students today would likely find learning in such an environment to be quite a challenge. (Courtesy of Michael C. Hardy.)

The school in Hawk was similar to other one- or two-room schools across the county: one- or two-room structures with a couple of teachers who taught as many students as showed up. Children brought their own lunches, and the only restroom facilities were outhouses. (Courtesy of the Morgan family.)

Pictured here is the starting lineup of the 1951 Bowman High School football team. From left to right are (first row) Ronnie Brummitt, right end; Jack Buchanan, right tackle; Wade Holder, right guard; Kenneth Phillips, center; Bruce Phillips, left guard; Bill Beline, left tackle; and David Vinson, left end; (second row) Bobby Thomas, quarterback; Jimmy McKinney, right halfback; Dickie Baker, fullback; and George Howell, left halfback. (Courtesy of the Bakersville Public Library.)

Harris High School's 1958 men's basketball team poses in the school gymnasium. From left to right are (first row) Lewis Biddix, Ray Biggerstaff, Tommy Phillips, Lanny Wilson, Sammy Buchanan, Larry Sparks, Mike Gouge, and David Deyton; (second row) Bobby Glenn (manager), Sale Duncan, Charles Hicks, Bobby McNeil, Scottie Roberts, Jimmy Young, Winston Hefner, Larry Sprinkle, and coach ? Norton. (Courtesy of Chris Hollifield.)

Three

FOOTPATHS, FERRIES, AND IRON HORSES
TRANSPORTATION

When the first settlers arrived in the Toe River Valley, the only transportation routes were footpaths. It took time to carve out roads big enough to accommodate a wagon. Most local citizens who did have wagons had multi-functional vehicles used for helping around the farm, for hauling produce to market, or for family excursions. Here members of the Burgan Gouge family are pictured taking their wagon up to Roan Mountain. (Courtesy of the Morgan family.)

In the 1950s and 1960s, school was seldom called off for "snow days." The snow had to be more than a foot, sometimes 2 feet deep, to necessitate a cancellation. Even then, if it snowed during the school day, the bus drivers, often older students, still had to deliver their students safely home. Pictured are the bus drivers for Harris High School in 1968: Scott Buchanan, Joe Stafford, Lawrence Glenn, Donald Stafford, Jimmy Burnett, and Reid Cox. (Courtesy of Chris Hollifield.)

Constructed by Baldwin Locomotive Works in 1883, engine No. 35 began life working on the Buffalo, New York, and Philadelphia Railroad. It was purchased by the South and Western Railroad and was transferred to the Clinchfield in 1908. This engine was scrapped in 1913. It is pictured here at the shops in Altapass in 1907. (Courtesy of John L. Burns.)

50

Prior to the advent of the steam-power shovel, all roads, whether they were intended for wagons, cars, or trains, were constructed by manual labor. Workers used shovels, pick axes, and dynamite to cut out the roadways. Steam shovels were powered by coal, just the same way steam locomotives were. While dynamite was used to break large boulders, the steam shovels moved much more rock and dirt than was ever possible by hand. This image shows a steam shovel working on the road between the railroad depot at Toecane and the county seat at Bakersville. (Courtesy of Louellen Peterson.)

When the South and Western Railway came into Mitchell County, the decision was made to bypass the county seat at Bakersville. The citizens at Bakersville lobbied vigorously to get the railroad in the town, but railroad officials chose to keep to the Nolichucky/Toe River area. The closest the railroad came to Bakersville was three miles. The town of Toecane sprang up at this point and became a hub of traffic coming and going to Bakersville. In the early 1900s, when the "good roads" policy was beginning to take effect, the first paved road in the area connected Bakersville with Toecane. However, instead of asphalt, concrete was used, as shown in these images. (Both, courtesy of Daniel Barron.)

Community development took off with the arrival of the Clinchfield Railroad. People could now travel to other parts of the United States, and they could sell their own produce and order items for their homes from all across the country. Sam Wilson, standing here by the depot in Toecane, was one of the many depot agents who made this new flexibility possible. (Courtesy of Daniel Barron.)

Before bridges were built, the only way to cross Mitchell County's rivers was to wade across at a ford or to use a ferry, as the four young ladies are doing in this image. Often ferry operators were given special licenses by the state. Here Jesse W. Rhyne uses a rope to pull his boat and passengers across the Toe River. (Courtesy of Doris R. Thompson.)

53

Not everyone was forced to ride in the farm's wagon when the time came to go to town or church. Some families could afford a separate buggy or "hack" for those special trips. Here Arthur and Mary Byrd, with their son Jack, are off on an excursion. (Courtesy of Rhonda Gunter.)

Engine No. 51 was built by Baldwin Locomotive Works for the South and Western Railroad in 1905. When the line became the Clinchfield Railroad in 1908, the engine became a Clinchfield locomotive. This photograph was made in Altapass in 1907. Sadly, this handsome engine was scrapped in 1938. (Courtesy of John L. Burns.)

Extensive logging took place throughout Mitchell County in the first half of the 20th century. While some logging companies used specialized locomotives, log loaders, and skidders, Champion Paper and Fiber Company employees, when they came to log on Roan Mountain, built a plank, or board, road on the mountain on which logging trucks could drive. When not in use by the company vehicles, the board road was used by locals. (Courtesy of the Morgan family.)

Prior to the state's taking over the maintenance of public roads in 1921, every able-bodied male was required to turn out and work on the roads once or twice a year. The two young men on the wagon are members of the Buchanan family working on the road in Kona. Interestingly, one can actually see the photographer and his camera in the shadow in the foreground. (Courtesy of Jerry Sullins.)

Commercial mining on a large scale required a great deal of specialized machinery. This was the first truck to work in the Big McKinney Mine, and it was driven by Clifton Smith. The truck was a solid-rubber-tire White model. (Courtesy of Emerald Village.)

As much as Toecane was the rail access for Bakersville, Green Mountain became the rail access for Burnsville in Yancey County. Materials were unloaded and taken by wagon, or later truck, to the county seat. In 1907, the Black Mountain Railroad was started, and in 1910, it reached Burnsville, eliminating the need for an overland route from the Green Mountain depot. (Courtesy of John L. Burns.)

56

In 1905, trains from the South and Western Railroad left Spruce Pine and could travel as far as Altapass. From October 1905 until September 1908, when the line was completed down the mountain to Marion, Altapass was the railhead of the railroad. This photograph shows the first passenger train in Altapass in 1906. (Courtesy of John L. Burns.)

In 1912, teams of men and animals began work on the Linville-to-Altapass section of the Appalachian Highway. The brainchild of state geologist Joseph Pratt, this ambitious project would link up several existing roads and, at times, make new ones to bring tourists to view the scenery and stay at local inns. The United States' involvement in World War I brought an end to the project. (Courtesy of Tense Banks.)

Hundreds of sites across Mitchell County have been mined for minerals like mica and feldspar. The Wisemans mined on Brushy Creek and Sullins Creek. This "dinky" line was used to haul the minerals out of the mine. By the looks of this image, pulpwood was also hauled on the line. Small spur lines were numerous all along the lines. (Courtesy of Russell and Mary Burleson.)

Early doctors did most of their work from horseback. A neighbor was often sent to the doctor with news of a sick or injured person. The doctor would mount his horse and ride, sometimes at night or in foul weather, to see to the ailing individual. All of the doctor's tools and medicines were carried in saddlebags. Here is Mitchell County's Dr. Virgil R. Butt astride his faithful form of transportation. His saddlebag full of medicine and instruments is visible just below his hand. (Courtesy of Daniel Barron.)

The railroad depot in Toecane in the 1950s also served as a Western Union telegraph office. Once the railroad ceased passenger traffic, the need for a depot became smaller and smaller. With better roads, deliveries were made by trucks. The railroad still runs through Mitchell County, but the trains no longer stop, save for on a siding while another train passes. (Courtesy of John L. Burns.)

With the arrival of the automobile in Mitchell County, taking rides in one of the newfangled contraptions was a novelty and an adventure. Pictured here are Nell Pittman and Lon Pittman in the backseat, while Will Burleson drives. This photograph was taken on Cane Creek, possibly beside the old Hawk School building. (Courtesy of the Morgan family.)

Passenger service on the local railroad ended in 1954. However, the old Clinchfield, now owned by CSX, is still one of the major rail lines between the coal fields of Kentucky and the Atlantic Coast. This photograph, taken in the 1960s, shows one of the long coal trains that snake their way down the mountain and into Spartanburg, South Carolina. (Courtesy of Daniel Barron.)

Kona was once a thriving town with numerous mica and feldspar producing facilities, along with stores, churches, and schools. The old Black Mountain Railroad used to branch off at Kona and headed to the lumber mills in Pensacola. The depot is pictured here in this mid-1950s photograph. (Courtesy of John L. Burns.)

Three

THE LOVED ONES AT HOME

FAMILY AND FRIENDS

The Dock Greene family was from Cane Creek near Bakersville. From left to right are (first row) Eva, Margie, and Dock Greene; (second row) Arbie, Jane, Bertie, Lula, and Arie. (Courtesy of Debra Cagle.)

Pictured here are members of the Young family. From left to right are (first row) Columbus Young; his wife, Sarah Ann David Young; Preston Young; Harriet Young Johnston; (second row) Jim Young; Arnold Young; Mamie Young Howell; Homer Young; and Carl Young. (Courtesy of Rhonda Gunter.)

Members of the Pannell family pose here in front of their home. From left to right are (first row) Harriett, Coleman, and Lorena Pannell; (second row) Ruth and Kathleen Pannell. (Courtesy of the Morgan family.)

Until well into the 20th century, pregnancy was seldom discussed, and even married women generally concealed their altered waistlines. Pictured here in 1917 are (from left to right) members of the Howell family of Rebel's Creek: Claude, Byrd, Ed, Bertha, and Herbert. Bertha was expecting her fourth child. It is unusual that she would have been photographed in her "delicate condition," but the rarity of a traveling photographer likely precluded the social taboo of appearing pregnant. (Courtesy of Ted Howell.)

When Don J. McKinney and his brother David Fillmore McKinney married, they married sisters, the daughters of Mack and Martha Young. David is pictured here with his second wife, Melissa. (Courtesy of the Morgan family.)

A native of Shelburne, Massachusetts, Dr. Ebenezer Childs was born in 1784. He moved to the area in the 1850s and died in 1862, just a year after Mitchell County was formed. His remains were placed in an alcohol-filled lead coffin and interred at Childsville, then serving as the county seat of government for Mitchell County under the name of Calhoun. Childs's remains were later removed to Elmwood Cemetery in Columbia, South Carolina. (Courtesy of the Avery County Historical Museum.)

Arnold McKinney was a carpenter, building houses all over Mitchell County. He was from the Young Cove area. As a child, Arnold helped out on a neighboring farm, rocking a baby while the women worked. The babe in the cradle was Carrie Young, whom Arnold later married. (Courtesy of the Morgan family.)

Members of the Sparks family were captured in this c. 1915 image. From left to right are (seated) Elizabeth Buchanan Sparks; (standing) Eli Stephen Sparks with his wife, Nancy Alica Duncan Sparks, sister Delia Sparks Miller, daughter Laura Sparks, and sister Susan Sparks. (Courtesy of Rhonda Gunter.)

Taken in 1902, this photograph shows a fine group of young ladies, apparently working on a quilt. They are, from left to right, (first row) Maude Young, Beanche Pritchard, Genevae Gudger, and Minnie Wilson; (second row) Inez Young, Bessie Anderson, unidentified, and Cary Bailey. (Courtesy of Daniel Barron.)

In 1968, the children of Fred and Norrie Sullins gathered at their home on Sullins Branch to celebrate the 69th wedding anniversary of their parents. Standing from left to right are Vinnie Sullins Buchanan, Rubbie Teal, Jess Sullins, Winnie Sullins Vance, Wait Sullins, Clyde Sullins, Lawson Sullins, and Gordon Sullins. Fred and Norrie can be seen on the porch behind their children. (Courtesy of Jerry Sullins.)

Julius Henline was one of the most beloved pastors of the county, working at Roan Mountain Baptist Church for 40 years. He is here with his family. From left to right are (first row) Cordie and Julius Henline; (second row) Walter, Paul, Bell, Ruth, and Claire Henline. (Courtesy of Darlene Wise.)

J. B. Craigmiles was one of those early-20th-century men who helped make Mitchell County what it is today. He came from Asheville to Bakersville and established a newspaper, the *Mitchell County Banner*, which he managed from 1914 to 1936. Craigmiles was also a justice of the peace, chairman of the Mitchell County chapter of the War Savings Campaign of 1918, and the owner of a boardinghouse at the time of his death. (Courtesy of Daniel Barron.)

In 1858, John B. Palmer moved from Detroit, Michigan, to what was then Watauga County. In 1861, his section became Mitchell County, and Palmer quickly became a leading member of the new county. He was appointed one of the commissioners to select a county seat and was an associate justice on the Court of Pleas and Quarter Sessions. He became colonel of the 58th North Carolina Troops during the Civil War. He left after the war and resided in Columbia, South Carolina. (Courtesy of Michael C. Hardy.)

This charming family portrait features John Esten Petersen, Jessie Rhyne Petersen, and their daughter Joyce Petersen Boone. J. E. Petersen was a Mitchell County merchant for many years with both a wholesale business and a Frito-Lay franchise. Jessie was a teacher in Mitchell County, and Joyce continues the family tradition of community involvement and education in her position at Mayland Community College. (Courtesy of Rhonda Gunter.)

The John Murdock family of Rebel's Creek includes, from left to right, (first row) unidentified, John Murdock, Ruth Owen, Ron Queen, and Woodrow Murdock; (second row) Jennie Grindstaff Murdock, Dessie Murdock Mason, George Murdock, Ammass Murdock, Florence Murdock Boone, and Ester Murdock; (third row) Texie Gouge Murdock, Vergia Murdock, Estel Murdock Howell, unidentified, and Bill Boone; (fourth row) unidentified, Seldon Murdock, and Oscar Murdock. (Courtesy of Ted Howell.)

In this 1890s portrait, Stokes Thomas Young (1882–1950) strikes a pose reminiscent of Teddy Roosevelt and his Rough Riders, whose Spanish-American War exploits captured the American imagination during the short but tense period of conflict. Though urban color writers would doubtless have classified this image as evidence of Appalachian violence, it instead demonstrates the region's connectedness with national and world events. Stokes was the son of Thomas and Harriet Gouge Young. (Courtesy of Rhonda Gunter.)

Dellinger Grist Mill is located in the Hawk community, just four miles east of Bakersville. The mill was established by this man, Reuben Dellinger, in 1867. Dellinger was from present-day Avery County, but he moved to Hawk following the Civil War. The Dellinger family still maintains and operates the mill. (Courtesy of the Morgan family.)

69

Joseph Ellis was born in 1828 while the area was still part of Burke County. His wife, Catherine Buchanan, was born in 1831. They were known in the community as "Uncle Joe and Aunt Katie." The couple had 17 children, of which 14 lived to adulthood. Joe's beard, which looks so distinguished here, was actually a fake one he tied on for special occasions. (Courtesy of Rhonda Gunter.)

This group of charming young ladies was photographed on Cane Creek about 1910 sporting fashionable clothing and hat styles of the period. From left to right are Bess McKinnie, Bertie Wilson, Hassie Haney, and Lou Wilson. There is also a fifth, unidentified, individual just visible in the window on the left. (Courtesy of Rhonda Gunter.)

This c. 1893 photograph of the James Wilson family was taken in the White Oak Community. Pictured from left to right are (first row) James, Bessy, Jane, Maggie, and Matty; (second row) Charlie, Laura, Johnson, and Albert. (Courtesy of Tom Wilson.)

Families have always used the parks along the Blue Ridge Parkway for special outings. Pictured here around 1957 at Crabtree Meadows is the "Uncle Pink" or "Uncle Turby" Turbyfield family. From left to right are Ora Harrison, Pearl Linebarier, Lillie Turbyfield, Pinkney "Pink" Turbyfield, Lillian Cox, and Effie Rhyne. In 1956, "Uncle Pink" had 24 grandchildren, 35 great-grandchildren, and 3 great-great-grandchildren. (Courtesy of Louellen Peterson.)

The son of Reuben and Mary Young, Moses Young had the unenviable job of being captain of the local home guard company during the Civil War. Captain Young was thus responsible for keeping law and order, and for taking care of the needs of Confederate widows, which included the distribution of food and salt. He lived on Cane Creek, operated a store, and did some mining. (Courtesy of Rhonda Gunter.)

World War I, or the Great War, was billed as the war to end all wars. Numerous Mitchell County men served in the different branches of the armed forces during the war. Here are two of them; Bill Peterson is on the left, with a painted backdrop. According to the note on the back of the right image, the gentleman with the real Sibley tents is Biss Wheeler (Silvers?). (Courtesy of Bud McKinney and Jerry Sullins.)

Arthur Woody, seen here caning the bottom of a chair with his daughter, Dicey Woody, came from a long line of chair makers. Arthur was born in 1856 and was still making chairs at the age of 95. He died in 1952. Arthur's father, Henry Woody, and his grandfather, Wyatte Woody, were also craftsmen, making chairs, wagons, and tables. (Courtesy of Woody's Chair Shop.)

Pictured here are members of the Reuben McKinney family from the White Oak community. Pictured from left to right are (first row) Reuben McKinney, Judy Burleson McKinney, Fred A. McKinney, and Minnie Lee Wiseman McKinney, holding Gwendolyn McKinney; (second row) four spinster sisters: Martha McKinney, Dovie McKinney, Lillian McKinney, and Beatrice McKinney. (Courtesy of Rhonda Gunter.)

Textile production was an important task for women like Nancy Sophia Young Blalock (1844–1895). Fibers, particularly wool, had to be cleaned, carded, and spun to make thread. In order to twist and pull the fibers into usable thread, women could use a small drop spindle or a large spinning wheel like this "walking" wheel, so named because the operator stood while using it. Nancy, whose parents were Rueben and Sophia Baker Young, was married to Confederate soldier Samuel Blalock. (Courtesy of Rhonda Gunter.)

At home, possibly on leave, Ralph H. Gunter strikes a jaunty pose. He served in the navy during the closing days of World War II, serving on board the USS *Guadalcanal*. The *Guadalcanal* was an aircraft carrier that hunted German submarines in the Atlantic Ocean. The ship earned three battle stars and a presidential citation for her actions during the war. (Courtesy of Rhonda Gunter.)

S. G. Brinkley, shown here in a publicity photograph, claimed to have the world's longest beard and even worked for a time in the circus. While he did not have the official world-record longest beard, at 5 foot, 4 inches, these were more than enough whiskers for most people. (Courtesy of Claudia McGough.)

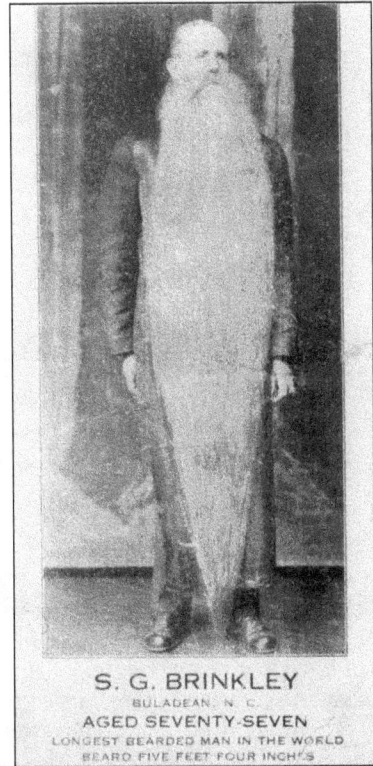

S. G. BRINKLEY
BULADEAN, N. C.
AGED SEVENTY-SEVEN
LONGEST BEARDED MAN IN THE WORLD
BEARD FIVE FEET FOUR INCHES

The Buchanan family was from Possum Trot. From left to right are (first row) Mattie Lee Howard, Ira Buchanan Jr., Terry Buchanan, and Geraldine Buchanan Ellis; (second row) Ira Buchanan, Edith Sparks Buchanan, Frank Sparks, Dolly Sparks, and Ruth Sparks Duncan. (Courtesy of Buster Sparks.)

William "Keith" and Malinda Blalock were some of the most colorful characters in the area during the Civil War. They both served in the Confederate army and later served as scouts for the Union army. After the war, they moved to Texas for a time and then returned to Bakersville, where Keith ran for state office. They later settled in Montezuma, where they are buried. (Courtesy of the Avery County Historical Museum.)

With their home as a backdrop, pictured here are members of the Deck McKinney family around 1920. From left to right are (first row) Jess McKinney, Jackie McKinney, Dexter Zeb "Deck" McKinney, and Celia Elizabeth "Lizzie" Young McKinney; (second row) Pearl McKinney, Bess McKinney, and Minnie McKinney. (Courtesy of Rhonda Gunter.)

Prior to World War I, the "Little Lord Fauntleroy" style of clothing was immensely popular throughout America. Based on the descriptions and illustrations in Frances Hodgson Burnett's beloved children's classic, the fashion included curled hair, a tailored suit with a wide lace collar, and short pants. Epitomizing the style is Ernest McKinney, son of Fonzer and Maggie Wilson McKinney, whose youthful charm is made more poignant by his short life, 1903–1920. (Courtesy of Rhonda Gunter.)

The Jeff Murdock family was from Rebel's Creek. From left to right are (first row) Jeff Murdock, James D. Howell, and Ester Murdock; (second row) Florence Murdock Boone. Like most babies in 1929, regardless of their gender, James is wearing a dress and would do so until he was toilet trained. This practice continued well into the mid-20th century, as it aided in changing the baby and made preparing clothes for a baby easier. (Courtesy of Ted Howell.)

The Peterson family chose the extensive garden surrounding their home in Poplar for their c. 1900 photograph. From left to right are (first row) L. Mary and Jonas Peterson; (second row) Goldie, Rosie, and Fannie Peterson. (Courtesy of Bud McKinney.)

This c. 1904 photograph, taken in Ledger, shows Phillips Wilson and his 10 sons. Almost all of these men were at least 6 feet tall. From left to right are (seated) Phillips, Wilburn, William, Reuben, and Lenn; (standing) Milton, Marion, Sidney, Henry, Mack, and Newton. (Courtesy of the Mitchell County Historical Society.)

Each community usually had someone who dabbled in photography. These men were not full-time artists. They simply had an interest and either inherited the equipment or purchased it via mail. Here, with his wife, Susan Freeman, and an unidentified granddaughter, is Bakersville photographer Fate Buchanan. Some of Buchanan's work was the subject of a book entitled *Appalachian Picture Man* (1989), edited by Ann Hawthorne. (Courtesy of Rhonda Gunter.)

The Toe River Valley has had more than its fair share of nationally known talent. One of the most popular acts was Lulu Belle and Scotty Wiseman. The couple performed regularly on WLS in Chicago. When at home in Avery County, they often played local benefit concerts in Mitchell County. Lulu Belle represented the area in the state legislature from 1975 to 1978. (Courtesy of the Avery County Historical Society.)

Although "color writers" and photographers from outside the region often tried to portray rural Appalachian people as cut off from the rest of the country, Mitchell County was far from isolated. Thanks to rail service and mail-order catalogs, local young men could keep up with fashions popular throughout the country, as this image of three dapper young men attests. Pictured in front is Fred Stewart, with Emmett Ellis (left) and Audie Miller in the back. (Courtesy of Buster Sparks.)

Mitchell County residents have fought in every conflict in which the United States has engaged. Such service often took local men far from home. One such individual was John Tipton, a veteran of the Mexican War (1846–1848), pictured here long after his military service far to the south. Although his walking stick stands at the ready, he poses proudly without its aid. (Courtesy of Rhonda Gunter.)

Tommy and Rachel Silver Thomas pose with a family Bible, a popular photographic prop. Tommy was a Confederate veteran. Rachel was a sister to the ill-fated Charlie Silver. (Courtesy of Helen McKinney.)

December 28, 1927, was a joyous day on Rebel's Creek. On that December day, Herbert and Estell Howell were wed at her parents' home. Herbert was a miner and then later a cabinet maker. While some weddings were held at churches, historically, many of the nuptials were held at the home of the bride. (Courtesy of Ted Howell.)

Pictured here is the Stacy Buchanan family. From left to right are (first row) Carrie, Stacy, Burnie, Delidia, unidentified, and Jerome; (second row) Lizzie, Holden, and Elam. Stacy Buchanan owned a mill in the Bakersville section of Mitchell County. (Courtesy of Louellen Peterson.)

Fred Sullins, here with his wife, Norrie, was known as the "Crazy Deputy." He was once sent to arrest a "dangerous" man and chose to go without a gun. He succeeded in bringing in his man. Sullins was a county deputy for seven years and a policeman in Spruce Pine. He also was a blacksmith and, after automobiles made their appearance, a machinist in Spruce Pine for 28 years. (Courtesy of Jerry Sullins.)

Andrew Wilkerson Sullins and his second wife, Margaret Wiseman Sullins, pose in a "touched up" image. Andrew was a private in Company A, 58th North Carolina Troops, during the Civil War. Following the war, he kept a store and hauled produce to McDowell and Rutherford Counties. In the 1870s, he was in charge of the Mitchell County poorhouse. He died in 1906, and Margaret passed in 1926. (Courtesy of Rhonda Gunter.)

The David Cornelius Buchanan family here poses in front of the family home. This picture was later "colorized," much to the dismay of Texie, whose dress was done in the wrong color. From left to right are (first row) Bertha, Texie, Rosie, Arlene, David, and Docia; (second row) Tyson, Farrell, and Clifton. (Courtesy of Debra Cagle.)

A traveling photographer would load his equipment upon a horse or wagon and travel around the community. He then took the glass-plate negatives back to his studio and made the images, returning the prints to the customers later. Pictured from left to right are Duncan Hise, with his arm around Lloyd Hise; Hattie Hise holding George; Lee Hise; Fred Hise; Grace Hise; and Glenn Hise, to the left of his mother. There are two unidentified children in the photograph. (Courtesy of Rhonda Gunter.)

Charles Smith Gunter (1882–1961) was a well-known businessman in Spruce Pine. In the early 1900s, he built the first mica concentration plant in Spruce Pine. His son and grandson, Carl Sr. and Carl Jr., operated Spruce Pine's Gunter Machine Shop for many years. (Courtesy of Rhonda Gunter.)

Five

DECORATION DAYS, FIRES, AND FESTIVALS
MEMORABLE EVENTS

The Fourth of July has always been an important holiday for people in Western North Carolina whose ancestors helped turned the tide of the American Revolution at the Battle of Kings Mountain. Here are members of a brass band from Spruce Pine who performed a concert on July 4, 1927. (Courtesy of Russell and Mary Burleson.)

In 1919, the town of Spruce Pine organized its first fire department with Jake Burleson as fire chief. Over time, the department grew from a hand-pulled cart to a 1929 Ford Model T, then a Dodge fire truck, and, in 1932, an American LaFrance. The October 1949 issue of the *Tri-County News* had this to say: "Latest available picture of Spruce Pine Fire Department with one of the two modern trucks operated by the department." (Courtesy of the Morgan family.)

The tide of the American Revolution was largely changed as a result of just one battle: Kings Mountain. The patriots who fought the British were known as the Overmountain Men. On September 29, 1780, the Overmountain Men passed through Gillespie Gap on their way to the battle. This marker was erected in 1930s to commemorate their passage through the Gap, which is in southern Mitchell County. (Courtesy of Michael C. Hardy.)

Fourth of July and Christmas parades have often been highlights of the year, bringing out people from all over the county. This 1949 Christmas parade in Bakersville shows the man of the moment, Santa Claus, handing out lollipops as he rides in a truck from Graham's Store, which sold furniture, hardware, and appliances. Customers could reach the store by dialing "13." The Northwestern Bank is in the background. (Courtesy of the Morgan family.)

Armistice Day, celebrated on November 11, honors the truce signed by the Allies and Axis powers that symbolically ended World War I. In this photograph, students have gathered in the street in Bakersville to celebrate the day. Since the end of World War II, Armistice Day has been known as Veterans Day. (Courtesy of Daniel Barron.)

Throughout the South, usually in the spring and summer, families gathered for "decoration day" at family or local church cemeteries. Family and community groups cleaned graves, placed flowers, and reconnected with relatives and friends. Often, churches had a dinner on the grounds at these decoration day activities. The above scene shows a decoration day at Bear Creek Baptist Church. (Courtesy of Buster Sparks.)

Charles McCartney, also known as the Goat Man, wandered the United States from 1930 to 1968 in a wagon pulled by a team of goats. Charles dressed himself and his son, Albert, in goat skins and survived on goat milk and the generosity of strangers or on money raised selling postcards or trinkets. The Goat Man visited Mitchell County in the 1950s. (Courtesy of Rhonda Gunter.)

Built in 1937, the Carolina Theater is a classic example of theater architecture. The 5,000-square-foot building showed movies on the silver screen and also featured live acts. In the late 1940s, O. D. Calhoun acquired ownership of the theater. He started a live music program entitled the *Carolina Barn Dance*. The Liberty Broadcasting Company of Dallas, Texas, soon began broadcasting the *Barn Dance* nationally on 512 different radio stations. The *Barn Dance* featured both local and national country music acts. Some of the well-known acts who played on the *Barn Dance* included Lulu Belle and Scotty, Chet Atkins, Bill Monroe, Patsy Cline, Hank Snow, Kitty Wells, and Sonny James. The *Carolina Barn Dance* ended in 1954 or 1955. The theater continued to show movies well into the 1990s. Then the building served as two different restaurants and two different churches. The historic site was purchased in 2004 and is undergoing restoration to once again serve the community. Live shows are again entertaining audiences at the Carolina Theater. (Courtesy of Michael C. Hardy.)

Folks traveling down the Blue Ridge Parkway can stop in and visit the historic Orchard at Altapass. The orchards were planted more than 100 years ago by the railroad company, and the trees continue to thrive, producing beautiful and delicious fruit. During the summer and fall, visitors can stop at the Orchard and hear good music, enjoy storytelling, or meet a local author. A trip to Mitchell County is incomplete without a visit to the Orchard at Altapass. (Courtesy of Michael C. Hardy.)

In October 1923, a fire swept through Bakersville, destroying a large portion of the town. One newspaper account made mention that at the Baker Brothers Garage, a car and a tractor were inside the garage and were lost to the fire. Perhaps this photograph documents that car and tractor. (Courtesy of the Morgan family.)

The Rhododendron Festival began in June 1947, a "two-day celebration to memorialize and perpetuate the most gorgeous display of natural beauty on the North American continent." The festival was originally held at the top of Roan Mountain, where numerous rhododendrons put on a spectacular display of blooms each year. This photograph, taken in 1959, features Jean Duckcroth (left) and Patianee Ray. (Courtesy of the Mitchell Historical Society.)

Good road access (internal improvements) has long been a topic of conversation. Citizens of Mitchell County wanted better access to Roan Mountain. On July 13, 1950, North Carolina governor Robert Cherry met with the Mitchell County Committee on Roan Mountain. Jeter Burleson, A. W. Phillips, John McBee, and S. T. Henry were some of the members of the committee. (Courtesy of Chris Hollifield.)

This assemblage of young men beside the courthouse in Bakersville was the second group of volunteers to leave for service in World War I. They met in 1917 to be photographed by T. S. Tipton, who gave his address as Toecane, North Carolina. Some of the enlistees' names are unknown. Among those pictured are (first row) Charlie Ramsey, Tane Greene, Talmadge Johnson, and ? Pitman; (second row) Carl Loven, Claude Johnson, Glenn Lawrence, John H. McKinney, and Jeff McKinney; (third row) Charlie Winters, Willard Buchanan, Avery Carpenter, George Johnson, and Bascom Parsons; (fourth row) Stokes McKinney, Homer McKinney, Lonzo Hall, ? Thomas, and Charlie Woody. Standing at the far left is Dr. ? Smith, medical examiner. Looking out the window on the right is D. W. Greene, superintendent of Mitchell County Schools. (Courtesy of Jerry Sullins.)

Traditionally, mountain people in need have been cared for by their families, neighbors, and churches. In the early 20th century, even before the implementation of federal welfare programs, the role of caring for the less fortunate was starting to become the prerogative of local and state governments. County homes were often established to provide for those unable to care for themselves. This image commemorates the August 13, 1922, services at the Mitchell County Home. (Courtesy of Louellen Peterson.)

Located on Beaver Creek Road, the Blue Marlin Swimming Pool was built in 1960 by Ralph Gunter. The purpose of the Olympic-size pool was to provide a place for the young people of Mitchell County to have recreational opportunities. During the 1960s and 1970s, the Red Cross taught numerous children to swim. (Courtesy of Rhonda Gunter.)

Located near Chalk Mountain, in Spruce Pine, the City Drive-In was the popular hangout place in the county in the 1950s. Customers could get barbeque, hamburgers, cheeseburgers, shrimp and fried chicken baskets, and malt shakes. Foot-long hotdogs and milk shakes were each only 30¢, quite a difference from fast-food prices today. (Courtesy of Chris Hollified.)

At mile marker 331, visitors can exit the Blue Ridge Parkway and visit the Museum of North Carolina Minerals. Opened in 1956, the museum was a joint project between the National Park Service and the North Carolina Department of Conservation and Development. In 2002, the museum was remodeled, and the exhibits were updated. The building also hosts a Mitchell County Chamber of Commerce Visitor Center. (Courtesy of Michael C. Hardy.)

Just before Christmas 1831, young Frances "Frankie" Stewart Silver claimed that her husband, Charlie, had disappeared. Although volunteers searched around the Silver homestead, one tracker, Jack Collis, eventually checked the cabin itself, including the fireplace, where he discovered bone fragments among the ashes. Over the next weeks, other portions of Charlie Silver's body were found, and each bit was buried when it was discovered. Thus Charlie Silver has three separate graves in this cemetery at Kona, where the three rough-hewn stones that mark the graves are visible in the foreground. A recent addition is a modern marker. Frankie was hanged in 1833 for the murder and dismemberment of her husband, but few historians feel she acted alone or in malice. Many believe she killed Charlie in self-defense and, panic-stricken, tried to get rid of the body, perhaps with help. However, only two people really know what happened in the Silvers' snow-bound cabin: one of them died with her story untold (the broadside ballad that bears her name was written by someone else and without her consent or input); the other lies in three graves by this picturesque church. (Courtesy of Michael C. Hardy.)

According to local tradition, early-19th-century Mitchell County legend Charlie McKinney was a man who liked women; he had at least four wives and 48 children who lived to adulthood. Apparently, the relationship between the members of this unusual arrangement all got along amicably. Each wife had her own homestead, and the large family all attended church together on Sundays. Because of this large brood, Charlie McKinney's Mitchell County descendants are legion, and few gatherings do not include at least one McKinney. The family has, of course,

intermarried with many other distinguished local families. This panoramic image captures the September 11, 1935, family reunion of the Woody and McKinney families at the Woody homeplace on Dale Road. No doubt Charlie McKinney would have been thrilled to see the nearly 75 lovely children gathered here around their elders. The older members of the family are seated on chairs at the center of the image, and several wear clothing that was likely fashionable in their youth. (Courtesy of Hazel Hollifield.)

It was a joyous occasion for the folks in the little village of Spruce Pine when their first bridge across the Toe River was completed. The date of this image is sometime around 1902, prior to the arrival of the railroad. Apparently, the bridge was lost during the 1916 flood that devastated Mitchell County. (Courtesy of Jerry Sullins.)

The bicentennial of America's birth in 1976 was celebrated from coast to coast. Special historical programs, fairs, festivals, train excursions, and plays were put on in just about every county. Here Edith W. Blevins and Charles Blevins appear in humorous costumes to prepare for Mitchell County's play. (Courtesy of the Mitchell County Historical Society.)

Brothers of the Bakersville Masonic Lodge around 1898 were, from left to right (first row) Bill Key, Jacob Bowman, Clayton Bowman, Christopher Garland, John S. Poteat, and Lace Byrd; (second row) Robert Young, Ephriam Clayton, Mitchell Buchanan, Will Bailey, Will Slagle, Charles Baker, and Henry Poteat; (third row) Joseph Turbyfield, Wesley Bailey, William Hawkins, S. J. Turner, Reuben J. Young, J. Clayton Bowman, and Sam Yelton. (Courtesy of the Morgan family.)

For many years, the annual Rhododendron Festival each June always featured a beauty pageant, culminating in the crowning of the Rhododendron Queen. Pictured here are the queen and her court from one of the festivals in the early 1970s. From left to right are Deborah Elaine Shook, third runner-up; Audrey Janey Thompson, second runner-up; Vicki Lynn Tunstall, queen; Cindy Kramer, first runner-up; and Victoria Lynn Henderson, fourth runner-up. (Courtesy of the Morgan family.)

Commencement has always been a day of great celebration. Pictured here are students from the Mitchell Collegiate Institute parading through the streets of Bakersville in September 1922. A brass band apparently leads the procession in front of the courthouse. However, the band was somewhat impeded in its progress by having to navigate through a street clogged with both automobiles and a team and wagon. (Courtesy of Daniel Barron.)

Historically, mountain families tended to be quite large. Many children were needed to help make a farm or business successful. In this October 1929 photograph, taken by a photographer from Asheville, the Stewart family, one of the oldest families in Mitchell County, posed for a photograph during their family reunion. The photograph was taken at the home of Doss Buchanan on Bear Creek. (Courtesy of the Morgan family.)

Six

HAYFIELDS, STORES, AND MICA
BUSINESS AND INDUSTRY

A group of miners poses in front of the famous Chestnut Flat Mine. From left to right, they are Ed Turbyfill, Arnold Blackburn, Jeff Willis, Merritt Sparks, John Duncan, Newland Sparks, Landon Pitman, Walter Buchanan, Ike Grindstaff, Roe Duncan, and Bob Duncan. Ground crystal from this mine was used to make the lenses for the telescope in Palomar, California. (Courtesy of Buster Sparks.)

Logging has been a mainstay in Mitchell County for decades. From left to right, Arvil Woody, David Williams, and Walter Woody move a log by hand onto the skids of a sawmill. The lumber the Woodys are moving was destined to become some of their world-famous chairs. A Woody chair is in the Smithsonian American Crafts Collection, and child-sized rockers, made for Caroline and John F. Kennedy Jr., are in the Kennedy Library. (Courtesy of Woody's Chair Shop.)

Young's Hotel was located in Bakersville and was a popular place to stay during court week. Lawyers often traveled via the railroad and, after a ride from Spruce Pine or Toecane, lodged for court week at Young's. While the lawyers engaged in heated debate in the courtroom, they could be seen companionably taking their meals together in the evenings. (Courtesy of Daniel Barron.)

Prior to World War II, mica could be imported from foreign countries more cheaply than it could be mined locally. With the advent of war, those foreign markets were closed, and the United States was forced to look toward its own natural resources. The government soon became the sole buyer of mica. The mineral could be found not only in every electrical component in every airplane, truck, and tank used by the U.S. military, but also in the eyeholes of gas masks, road goggles, and armored car peep holes. Western North Carolina supplied the majority of the mica used; old mines were reopened and new mines dug to extract the mineral. Countless jobs were created in an economy slow to recover from the Great Depression. These operations continued on through the Korean War. Pictured above in about 1955 is the mica depot established by the government in Spruce Pine. The photograph below shows young ladies grading the clarity of the mica. (Both, courtesy of Darlene Wise.)

Farmers often looked to technology to help them grow and harvest better crops from their farms. Regardless of what machinery they used, farmers relied heavily on their indispensable helper: the mule. Here Don J. McKinney rides on a hay/wheat cutter being pulled by a fine-looking set of mules. (Courtesy of Rhonda Gunter.)

In this Bayard Wooten photograph, community weavers gather at the Penland Weaving Cabin with their finished products. They met weekly to receive materials for new projects and to learn new weaving patterns and techniques from Lucy Morgan (1889–1981), founding director of the Penland Weavers and Potters and the Penland School of Crafts. (Courtesy of Penland School of Crafts.)

George Baker's store in Bakersville was a gathering spot for many of the locals. Among the many items sold at the store were Brown's Shoes. Not only does the large sign over the door advertise the shoes, but there are signs in the windows as well. The store was located right beside the meeting place of the International Order of the Odd Fellows. (Courtesy of Daniel Barron.)

The beehive-shaped iron smelting ovens of the Cranberry Coal and Coke Company can be seen here on the right. The iron deposits at Cranberry were mined as far back as the late 1700s. From 1861 until 1911, Cranberry was in Mitchell County. In 1911, the area became a part of North Carolina's youngest county, Avery. (Courtesy of the Caldwell Historical Museum.)

Completed in 1885, Cloudland Hotel sat atop Roan Mountain. The hotel, straddling the Tennessee–North Carolina line, was built by Union general John Wilder. Alcohol could only be sold and consumed on the Tennessee side of the building. Many American politicians and members of European royalty visited Cloudland. As a result of the high cost of maintaining the hotel, the building was abandoned in 1910, and the building materials were later auctioned off. (Courtesy of the Morgan family.)

The earliest forms of industry in the mountains, and the most important, were mills. Many water-powered mills turned grinding stones to which local inhabitants could take their wheat and corn and have them turned into flour for bread. Other mills powered machinery that ran saws. This mill, belonging to Stacy Buchanan, was located on Cane Creek near Bakersville. (Courtesy of Louellen Peterson.)

One of the earliest industries in Mitchell County was saw milling. Trees could be taken from the abundant forest and hauled to the sawmill to produce lumber either for one's own home or for sale. Pictured here in 1903 is the Dave Dellinger sawmill in the Hawk community. Oxen are being used to drag the large logs to the steam-powered saw. (Courtesy of the Morgan family.)

Master chair maker Arthur Woody and his daughter, Decie, demonstrated chair seating during a 1930s Weaving Institute at Penland. Lucy Morgan (standing center) observed the Woodys. She is wearing a smock hand-woven and sewn by the Penand Weavers and Potters. (Courtesy of Penland School of Crafts.)

Flume lines such as this one, seen at a mine on the left-hand fork of the Pigeon Roost Creek, helped miners move their minerals long distances. This flume was small. Some flumes were large enough to move trees. (Courtesy of Faye Griffith.)

It is unclear just where this photograph was taken, possibly on Cane Creek. What is clear is that this is a rare photograph of a mica mine. Men climbed down a ladder into the shaft. Minerals, such as the large piece of mica being held aloft by the man in the center, were brought back to the surface using the winch. Mining like this took place all over the Toe River Valley. (Courtesy of the Morgan family.)

There were many enterprising individuals in Mitchell County, including Mike White, pictured here in his apron with some of his customers. White operated a café and sandwich shop in Bakersville. Customers could get a hot or cold lunch at any time, and they could even get ice cream. (Courtesy of the Morgan family.)

With the rise of the automobile and the construction of better roads, people began to travel for entertainment, especially after World War II. Small hotels and restaurants sprang up everywhere, catering to the needs of tourists. This hotel, the Bakersville Motel and Restaurant, is featured in this 1950s-era postcard. (Courtesy of Pack Memorial Library.)

This is *c.* 1910 Spruce Pine. The railroad had just recently arrived, and the town had started to grow. The large store on the right was a general store operated by the English family. There appears to be a telegraph office next door. The English family store was not the first in Spruce Pine. There was a store operated by L. A. Berry in 1903. (Courtesy of Rhonda Gunter.)

In 1918, the Harris Clay Company constructed a dam to supply power to its mining facilities at Sparks. At the insistence of people in Spruce Pine, a line was strung to the town. Harris Clay sold the "electric system" that powered Spruce Pine to Carolina Power and Light Company in 1926. Here Jesse Rhyne stands in front of the dam on the Toe River. (Courtesy of Louellen Peterson.)

The courthouse in Bakersville has been witness to many important aspects of Mitchell County history. Built in 1907, the building has been described by architectural historians as, "a compact Neoclassical Revival building of stuccoed concrete block." The Mitchell County courthouse is almost identical to a courthouse in neighboring Yancey County. Recently, the judicial system of Mitchell County moved to a new structure, and the old courthouse is on its way to becoming a first-class museum. (Courtesy of Rhonda Gunter.)

As in many other areas in the mountains of Western North Carolina, tourism played an important part of Mitchell County's economic development. Numerous inns and hotels sprang up, especially prior to the Great Depression. Pictured here is the Toplift Hotel, which also served as a bus station. The building was lost to a fire in 1948. (Courtesy of Daniel Barron.)

In the first couple of decades of the 20th century, North Carolina had a system of prison trustees for well-behaved inmates who had served most of their sentences. These men could be leased to private corporations for work crews. Convicts worked in the mines, on the railroads, or, as this photograph demonstrates, on road construction gangs. Unfortunately, many of these convicts were African Americans, and residents who had encountered few individuals not of European descent sometimes gained a negative impression of all African Americans. (Courtesy of the Morgan family.)

The craftsmen at Woody's Chair Shop have always been innovative. Walter Woody is seen here turning the legs for one of the family's world-famous chairs. The lathe is powered by an electric motor from an old elevator that was in a granary beside the railroad in Spruce Pine. The motor is many decades old and still works splendidly in the production of custom chairs, tables, bowls, and even pet caskets. (Courtesy of Woody's Chair Shop.)

112

The interior of the Spruce Pine Pharmacy and Dr. Charles A. Peterson's office are both shown here. In 1932, Peterson would "generously donate" the use of some space to the newly organized Central Baptist Church. According to the church's historian, lights, fans, "comfortable seats, and a nice pulpit" were installed, and another local couple let the new congregation use their piano. The church's first building was constructed from 1933 to 1937 and was located on Oak Avenue. (Courtesy of Rhonda Gunter.)

Found among the collections of the Mitchell County Historical Society, this photograph has unclear origins. It might have been taken in a chair making or other woodworking facility. Written on the back in faint pencil is the following information about the subjects: "B. C. Grindstaff, Pat Hailman, Chas. Hensley, Hershel Bumgarner, Marcillus Buchanan, and Graham Grindstaff." (Courtesy of the Mitchell County Historical Society.)

Not only was J. B. Craigmiles owner and editor of the *Mitchell County Banner*, he also operated a boardinghouse. Before hotels became prominent, it was not uncommon for local citizens to open their homes to visitors. After the death of Craigmiles, the house became known as Stewart Greene's Boarding House. The home was razed about 1981. (Courtesy of Daniel Barron.)

John Webb's General Store served Mitchell County citizens in the Brummett's Creek area. This c. 1936 photograph shows the employees of the store. From left to right are (first row) John Webb, Anna Webb, Pauline Webb, Fred Bryant, Francis Bryant, Howard Harrell, and Henry Thomas; (second row) ? Thomas, Lee Whitson, Troy Johnson, Oscar Renfro, Lester Webb, Thurman Webb, and Tom Webb. (Courtesy of Rhonda Gunter.)

Streets in towns were often a mixture of mud and manure. At times, especially during spring rains, these streets could be almost impassable quagmires. To improve the situation, rocks were ground into gravel and spread on the roads. Of course, this process had to be repeated frequently. Here a horse-drawn wagon hauls rocks to be crushed into gravel for a street in Bakersville. (Courtesy of Louellen Peterson.)

At one time, motorists needing assistance could contact Phillips and Coulter Motor Company 24 hours a day. Their shop, located in Spruce Pine, could overhaul motors and radiators, change oil, lubricate the chassis, and even wash cars. Their tow truck also provided valuable advertising of their services. (Courtesy of Daniel Barron.)

Often stores in communities across Mitchell County had dual functions. The store portion was where locals traded items grown on their farms for items they could not manufacture, like sugar and coffee. Many stores also served as post offices, as the Peterson Store in Poplar did. Here Brisco Peterson is standing in front of the Peterson Store. The wooden walkway stretched to the railroad tracks. (Courtesy of Bud McKinney.)

Emma Conley (left) and Lucy Morgan watch a dye pot. Before the importation of commercial dyes, mountain weavers and spinners used a variety of plants and other natural items for dyes and mordants. For nearly 20 years, beginning in the 1930s, Emma Conley taught spinning and dyeing with natural materials during Penland's summer craft sessions. She was a member of the Southern Highland Craft Guild and often demonstrated at guild fairs. (Courtesy of Penland School of Crafts.)

A photographer bravely climbed on top of a freight car to snap this image of Spruce Pine. It is unclear if the large gathering of people was a special occasion or just a day of normal business. It is interesting to notice how the tracks run on either side of the depot in the center of the picture. Today they are just on the left side. (Courtesy of Rhonda Gunter.)

In 1946, two World War II veterans set up shop near the Grassy Creek section of Mitchell County. Arvil Woody ran a grocery and gas station, while Walter Woody, not pictured, built chairs in the back. Eventually, the store portion was phased out, and the business became solely devoted to the production of chairs and other fine furniture. Pictured here are, from left to right, Ed Woody, Martin Woody, and Arvil Woody. (Courtesy of Woody's Chair Shop.)

Feldspar mined in the Toe River Valley area was used as a cleaning powder and in ceramics for the electrical industry. It also adds strength to pencils when combined with graphite. Pictured here is the Old Tennessee Minerals feldspar processing plant in Spruce Pine. The plant was later owned by Indusmin and KT Feldspar. (Courtesy of Rhonda Gunter.)

Gradually, the community's service station replaced the general store as the place to gather and discuss the happenings of the day, from local to national news. Chance's Texico Station was located in Bakersville. Pictured from left to right are Jess Leford (standing), store owner Luther Chance, and Morris Wilson. (Courtesy of the Morgan family.)

Mining has been a staple of Mitchell County's economy ever since the end of the Civil War. Mica, feldspar, and kaolin have been successfully taken from the ground and used in a variety of products from personal hygiene items, to cleaning products, to sophisticated technology. This photograph of an unidentified mine was taken by local photographer Jim Jones. Evident are the electricity used to power equipment inside the mine and the wooden flume used to transport materials out of the mine. (Courtesy of Daniel Barron.)

Located on Summitt Street in Spruce Pine, Bob and Gloria's Dairy Barn was a popular hangout, attested to by the number of cars seen here sitting in front of the establishment. This 1950s photograph shows that young people, as jobs turned from agriculture to industry, had time and money to spend socializing. (Courtesy of Rhonda Gunter.)

Early sawmills were water or steam powered. Later, as gasoline engines became available, they were put to use in the mill. The Woody family, makers of custom furniture, has innovatively used the front clip of a 1945 Buick, engine and all, to power their sawmill. The 1945 Buick had a straight-eight cylinder. The late Walter Woody is working on squaring up a log. (Courtesy of Woody's Chair Shop.)

The blacksmith was a vital part of the community. He manufactured items that were essential on the farm but could not be easily produced by most individuals. He also fixed broken items with his forge, anvil, and hammer. Pictured here is Wilson Smith Jones, a blacksmith who worked in Bakersville, with the tools of his trade. (Courtesy of Rhonda Gunter.)

Lucy Morgan and Howard C. "Toni" Ford posed next to the "Travelog," a portable shop for displaying and selling items produced by the Penland Weavers and Potters. In the summer of 1932, Toni Ford constructed the small log cabin on a truck bed. This unique motorized cabin was driven intact from Penland to Chicago, where it became part of an outdoor exhibition at the 1932 Chicago World's Fair. (Courtesy of Penland School of Crafts.)

Remnants of the old Clinchfield Railroad abound in Mitchell County. Old cabooses can be found on Altapass Road near the Vance Tunnel and on Halltown Road, and there is still a depot in Spruce Pine. A few of the old bridges, still in use by CSX, bear the old logo, as seen in this photograph taken near Relief. (Courtesy of Michael C. Hardy.)

The lunchroom staff of Bowman High School in 1963 served hot meals for the students, faculty, and staff. From left to right are Jayne Harrell, Mertal Byrd, Dolly Griffith, Helen Whitson, and Etta Mae Whitson. (Courtesy of the Bakersville Public Library.)

This rarity was photographed in the 1950s: this two-hole, two-door privy served passengers at the depot in Altapass. A rare treat was the vent pipe on the top to provide fresh air. Behind the privy is a railcar with a faded "Clinchfield" on the side. (Courtesy of John L. Burns.)

The old Clinchfield Railroad stretched from Elkhorn City, Kentucky, to Spartanburg, South Carolina. Along the way, the track traveled through 54 tunnels, an engineering feat even with modern technology, and most of these tunnels are 100 years old. This photograph is looking at the south end of the Vance tunnel. (Courtesy of John L. Burns.)

Lucy Morgan observed the community log-raising for the Edward F. Worst Craft House in May 1935. The Craft House was named for Penland's first weaving instructor, Edward F. Worst (1866–1949), a master weaver and public school educator from Chicago who taught at Penland most summers from 1929 to 1948. (Courtesy of Penland School of Crafts.)

Just about everything a person needed was available at Young's Store. One could purchase seeds, hats, Quaker Oats, Wheaties, Planters Peanuts, rain slickers, cigars, and just about anything else a person might need. George Young stands in front with an unidentified client behind him. (Courtesy of Daniel Barron.)

Gunter's Machine Shop was located in Spruce Pine. The shop was operated by Carl Gunter Sr. and then by Carl Gunter Jr. for many years. (Courtesy of Chris Hollifield.)

Spruce Pine's Oak Street, also known as "Upper Street," is pictured here in the 1950s. On Upper Street, one could get lunch and ice cream, then shop for groceries, appliances, or auto parts. (Courtesy of Pack Memorial Library.)

Even families who lived in town, like this Bakersville couple, often kept livestock. A horse could be used to haul loads, pull wagons, and power a plow for the garden every family had. Chickens, like those seen here, were useful not only for food, but also as an important business investment. Eggs and chickens were always a valuable asset that could be traded for a variety of products. (Courtesy of the Morgan family.)

This crew was employed in constructing the Tipton Hill school as part of a Works Progress Administration project. In addition to supplying the county with a well-built and beautiful school, the construction provided much-needed employment for local men who were hired to complete all phases of the project. (Courtesy of Rhonda Gunter.)

These gentlemen, Will Cook (left) and J. B. Jones, were two of Bakersville's first taxi drivers in the 1930s. With the nearest railroad depot three miles outside town, taxi drivers had plenty of work. Visible behind them and their well-polished taxi is the only movie theater Bakersville ever had. (Courtesy of Daniel Barron.)

BIBLIOGRAPHY

Adams, Kevin. *North Carolina Waterfalls*. Winston-Salem, NC: John F. Blair Publishers, 2005.

Bailey, Lloyd. *Toe River Valley Heritage*. Seven volumes. Durham, NC: L. R. Bailey, 1994–2008.

Bishir, Catherine, Michael Southern, and Jennifer Martin. *A Guide to the Historic Architecture of Western North Carolina*. Chapel Hill: University of North Carolina Press, 1999.

Goforth, James A. *Building the Clinchfield*. Erwin, TN: Gem Publishers, 1989.

Hardy, Michael C. *Remembering Avery County*. Charleston, SC: The History Press, 2007.

Laughlin, Jennifer Bauer. *Roan Mountain: A Passage of Time*. Johnson City, TN: Overmountain Press, 1999.

Lonon, J. L. *Tall Tales of the Rails: On the Carolina, Clinchfield, and Ohio*. Johnson City, TN: Overmountain Press, 1989.

Presnell, Lowell. *Mines, Miners, and Minerals of Western North Carolina*. Boone, NC: Parkway Publishers, 2005.

Rusher, Tom. *Until He is Dead: Capital Punishment in Western North Carolina*. Boone, NC: Parkway Publishers, 2003.

Sheppard, Muriel Earley. *Cabins in the Laurel*. Chapel Hill: University of North Carolina Press, 1935 and 1991.

Visit us at
arcadiapublishing.com